The Gardens of Florence Everts

The Gardens of Florence Everts

Preface by Adrian Higgins

The Gardens of Florence Everts

PUBLISHER
Spacemaker Press, LLC
James G. Trulove, Publisher
1250 28th Street, NW
Washington, DC 20007
202-257-5959

ISBN 978-0-9824392-4-1

Printed in China

First printing, 2010

1 2 3 4 5 6 7 8 9 / 11 10 09

Acknowledgements

This book, which presents a selection of my work over the past three decades, offers the opportunity to acknowledge and thank the persons who have been an influence and help in my professional life and in the preparation of this book.

First I wish to thank and to acknowledge the invaluable input over the years of Dennis Dixon and Susanne Fyffe, two landscape architects whose talent and skills have made an important contribution to so many of these projects. Their professionalism has been instrumental in sustaining the quality of the firm's work and their friendship has added immensely to the pleasure of the creative and practical process.

There are those I recognize and must thank for their assistance in the preparation of this book: Don Partlan, landscape architect, for his advice, patience, sound judgment and remarkable technological skills in dealing with the organization of the images; Marilyn Clemens, Darcy Foley, Mindy Kim and Robert Bolton for their excellent editorial assistance; James Trulove for the handsome design of this book.

This is also the place to mention some of those people whose encouragement and support have been an important influence over the years. Mina Hilsenrath, Chief of Resource Conservation for Howard county, Md., outstanding teacher, mentor and friend from my days as a student of landscape architecture at University of Massachusetts. Carolyn Revelle Hufbauer, Urban Planner, former director of the Landscape Design program at George Washington University and Karen Kumm, Urban Designer, Maryland National Capital Parks and Planning Commission, for their friendship, generous advice and counsel. I would also like to recognize the ten valuable years spent as partner of Martha Donnelly in our firm of Donnelly, Everts Associates. Here it seems appropriate to mention that I had the good fortune to have a father who was a devoted gardener.

And, of course, a debt of gratitude is due to the many supportive and imaginative clients. In particular however, I wish to acknowledge and thank the late Ambassador Walter Hummel and Mrs. Hummel and Ambassadors Ronald Spiers and Robert Oakley and their wives whose vision and continued persistence and interest over some years was responsible for the creation of a garden for the official residence of the American ambassador in Islamabad, Pakistan.

Contents

Preface

It has become a cliched observation of garden writers, railing against the lack of plantsmanship among landscape architects, that the profession reduces plants to the level of building blocks. Shrubs, hedges, trees are just additional elements to use in shaping spaces, as malleable and functional as fences or patios. The indictment continues: The designers don't know their plants, and seem to believe that those that they do, miraculously, neither grow nor die.

Like all stereotypes, this view never quite marries with reality. I know many landscape architects with a deep knowledge and love of plants. And then there is Florence Everts. Florence is an extraordinarily skilled and wise creator of landscapes who puts her client's requirements at the fore, masters the inevitable technical challenges of each project, and pulls it all together in a joyful tribute to the goddess Flora. When I think of Florence, I think of her first as a gardener, but only because she is such a good gardener. She was using variegated hakone grass in Washington before it was known here, along with the long neglected and sublime royal azalea, Rhododendron schlippenbachii.

Beyond her repertoire, and her formidable horticultural knowledge, Florence has an innate sense of the character of a plant, and how that can be used to effect the mood she is seeking.

The gardens featured here, while existing in the context of the lush Mid-Atlantic region, are wildly different. Contrast the sun-baked rooftop overlooking the National Mall to the quiet woodland of the Virginia piedmont. And yet through Florence's eye, each project shares a quality that is often sought by designers but rarely achieved. The land is altered and yet in a way that brings out its latent beauty and spirit. The only thing Florence imposes on a landscape is her genius. Hers is the hand of revelation.

There is no better example of this than the garden she has built for herself and her husband Stocky in Northwest Washington. She took a site with the twin liabilities of deep shade and impossible gradient and turned a sad hillside into a lyrical horticultural opera. One journeys through it—where vignettes trigger little Shangri-La moments—or one views it from the house in all its layered richness. I view it too as a shrine to the art of the landscape designer.

—Adrian Higgins

Adrian Higgins writes about horticulture, garden design and the environment for the Washington Post. *He is the author of* The Secret Gardens of Georgetown *and* A Guide to Chanticleer Garden, *to be published by the University of Pennsylvania Press in 2011.*

Introduction

"No occupation is so delightful to me as the culture of the earth, and no culture comparable to that of a garden."
—Thomas Jefferson

"What have you done with the garden that was entrusted to you?"
—Antonio Machado Spain 1875 - 1939

A garden is like no other art form, ever changing and ephemeral. For the designer, planning a garden is a continuous learning process due to this inherent element of change. The photographs provided in this book capture moments in the life of eleven widely different landscapes, from a six-acre garden for the American Embassy in Pakistan to a small rooftop garden overlooking Washington, DC, illustrating the breadth of work in a long career.

Many of these gardens grew out of neglected, barren sites. And this is essentially the art of landscape architecture—to be able to imagine, when faced with chaotic, imperfect conditions, how to reorder the landscape and create a new experience of nature, one that is both harmonious with the site and fulfills the owner's aspirations. Behind their design is the belief that a garden's real success lies in creating not only a beautiful setting, but also a functional and inviting background for living.

Planting design is at the heart of landscape architecture. A dynamic balance must be struck between hard surface features and the texture, color and variability inherent in the softness of the landscape. Successful spaces of all sizes retain both tension and balance between soft and hard elements and express a memorable sense of 'place.' Unlike the architect who may assume his building will remain unchanged, the landscape architect recognizes that change is inevitable, caused by man or the forces of nature. For the gardener, whether designer or client, watching a garden grow and change can be of endless interest and joyful anticipation. But a garden is managed nature, and its vitality depends on continuous attention, without which any design can vanish and return to nature, quickening the pace of this art towards the ephemeral.

—Florence Everts, ASLA

Washington, DC

Everts Garden

Washington, DC

Situated across from a woodland reserve, this house had an atmosphere of seclusion and quiet and despite its desolate landscape, it was the home my husband and I had hoped to find. But it came with challenges. From the street, the front garden consisted of an indifferent lawn with a lone River birch and at the rear, much of the land was a steep hillside that would demand unique solutions to transform a nearly vertical slope into a garden one could enjoy.

The design decisions for the front were straightforward. The birch tree was removed and the ground leveled with the creation of a low dry stone wall. A stone path with shallow steps was added from the curb to the house. In spring, one walks to the front door under a canopy of delicate pink dogwoods along a path lined with sequentially flowering crocus, daffodils, tulips, scillas, pulmonarias and forget–me-nots, all set against an evergreen backdrop.

But beyond the garden gate there were more significant difficultires in how to address the issues of grade, potential erosion, and access to the vertical slope that rose straight up from a lower terrace. Smothered in brambles, the hillside had no point of entry, so the first task was to build stone steps. Breaking into the existing six-foot retaining wall was a concern; this was addressed by designing the steps parallel to the wall to act as a buttress. The design of its wood balustrade was inspired by one seen in China.

Erosion is an ever-present concern when creating a garden on a steep slope. Rather than removing all the wild vegetation at once, the site was cleared incrementally leaving much of the fibrous root material. The planting was done in stages, allowing time for the new roots to take hold and over time the dense planting has effectively bound the soil to control erosion. The tempo of creating ones own garden allows time for nature to participate.

Gradually, winding paths of quarry boulders and low mossy walls of weathered fieldstone were added. In keeping with the site's informality, none of the walls run the entire width of the property, helping to integrate the garden into the hillside. But the focal point of the hillside garden

LEFT: *Dogwoods frame the path to the front door.*
ABOVE: *'Casablanca Lilies,' 'Carefree Roses' and Cone flowers bloom in the narrow side garden. Across the flagstone path inset with river stones, espaliered 'Snow Flurry' camellias alternate with 'Dee Runk' boxwoods. Fall blooming Begonia grandis edges the path.*

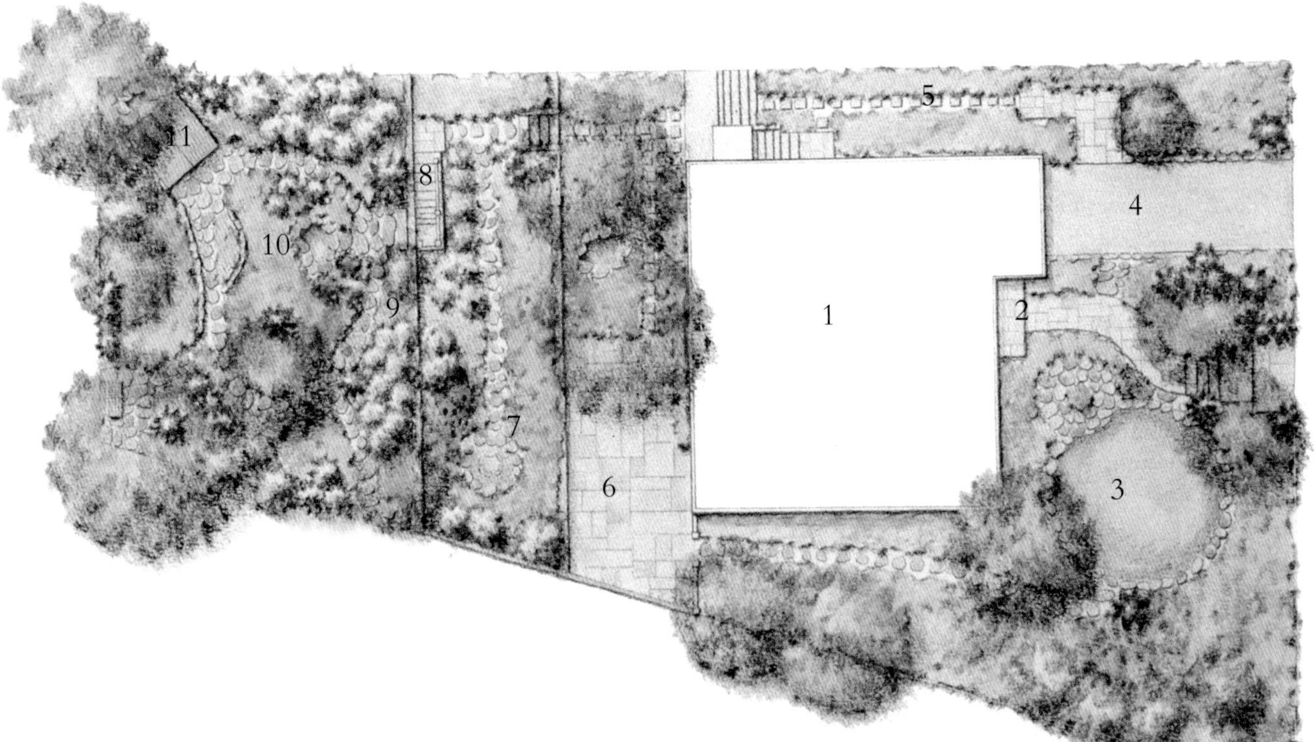
1
2
3
4
5
6
7
8
9
10
11

is a rustic Japanese-inspired tea house located at the very top of the slope which provides a destination from which to enjoy the view over the garden or as a restful place to sit in contemplation. Ascending the hillside hints at the classic Japanese principle of creating a microcosm of nature in a small space through the sequencing of different scenes to be discovered and enjoyed as the beholder continues his stroll. Since most of the hillside is shaded by neighboring pines, shade tolerant plants were selected, such as mahonias, rhododendrons, pieris, kalmia, azaleas and leucothoes as well as epimedium, woodland phlox, Himalayan Sweet Box, ferns and hosta.

The lower terrace garden, framed by pink and white dogwoods, is reached by a few steps up from the living room patio. It features a path of quarry flagstone and river washed pebbles. Edged by dwarf Kingsville boxwood and in spring, plantings on either side of tulips, pansies, scillas and astilbes in a pastel palette, complement the dogwoods and make a delicately colored scene from indoors. Seen from the tea house or the patio, Washington DC's rich spectrum of plant hues and textures is played out over the year.

FAR LEFT: *Section through the hill-side.*
LEFT: *A flagstone circle inset with river stones surrounded by 'Kingsville' boxwood terminates the path.*
BELOW LEFT: *Plan view of garden.*
RIGHT: *A rustic terrace walk in spring is lined on either side with 'Angelique' and 'Mt. Tacoma' tulips, blue pansies, forget-me-nots, scillas, and pulmonarias beneath a dogwood canopy.*

1. House
2. Entrance path
3. Circular lawn
4. Driveway
5. Side garden with stepping stone paths
6. Patio off living room
7. Elevated garden terrace
8. Steps to hillside
9. Retaining wall
10. Densely planted hillside with boulder steps
11. Rustic Japanese style pavilion

BELOW: *The patio in early summer is edged with white clouds of 'Strawberry Begonia' (Saxifraga stolonifera) in bloom under rhe branches of an old dogwood.*

BELOW: *The hillside in autumn.*
RIGHT: *A cascading azalea with a Rex begonia marks the stairway to the hillside.*

LEFT: *Boulder steps with unpeeled 'post and rope' railing lined with 'Graham Blandy' boxwood and mixed plantings of perennials and shrubs.*

ABOVE: *The shingle roof of the tea house is supported by posts of unpeeled cherry resting on stone seat walls. The floor is paved with quarry flagstone and river pebbles.*
RIGHT: *Informal plantings densely planted on the steep slope blend with the woodland setting.*

Spencer Garden

Washington, DC

LEFT: *Dining terrace as seen from the stepping stone path.*
ABOVE: *View back to the building from the terrace.*

Entering this ground floor apartment from a busy thoroughfare in downtown Washington, DC, one is not prepared for the cool enchantment of a shaded courtyard garden that lies at the rear of this old high-rise building.

Moving to the city after having always enjoyed the pleasure of living with a large garden, the owner was attracted to this condominium for its outdoor space. Despite the fact that its ground plane was completely covered with wood decking, and of an unusual shape, it was redeemed by the existence of old mature Bradford pear trees that provided shade and created a sense of enclosure and privacy from the building above. The client, believing a garden is restorative amidst the pressures and noise of city living, looked forward to having a terrace for entertaining and a swimming pool for exercising.

The first step in this challenging assignment was the demolition of the wood decking which concealed sharp grade changes beneath. Large amounts of fill were required to create a level surface. Access to the site was limited; all construction materials and plants had to be brought in by hand or wheelbarrow. The irregular shape of the space proved to be an advantage, making it possible to create two distinct and separate spaces: one, a large open area visible and accessible from the living room and the other, a smaller secluded space sited around the corner of the building. Hidden from view from the rest of the garden, this was the ideal location for the installation of an exercise swimming pool.

Today the site has been transformed into a lush garden with subtle changes in elevation. The Bradford pears have been radically pruned to admit light. From the living room, French doors open to a wide landing with shallow steps down to a generous terrace with curving seat walls. Level with the landing, a raised bed features an elegant Japanese maple planted with Asian gingers and 'Pewter Veil' heucheras beneath its delicate canopy. Stepping stone paths lead from the terrace through beds planted with a variety of shade-loving plants, such as hellebores, ferns, hostas, and sarcoccoca.

In a far corner of the garden, a waterfall splashes into an ornamental pool. A fence surrounds the garden designed with mirror-backed lattice panels, which, by reflecting more light, creates the illusion of open space beyond. At night, lights hidden high in the trees throw dappled shadows below. Camellias thrive, planted against the fence and walls of the building. Off to one side, a low gate draws the eye toward the entrance of the space where the 'endless' pool is tucked away from view.

This secluded garden has not only become a source of pleasure for the client, offering a refuge from city noise, it has also expanded her living space, and provided an inviting setting for her frequent social gatherings.

1. Living room
2. Landing
3. Steps
4. Terrace
5. Pool with waterfall
6. Seat wall
7. Stepping stone path
8. Gate
9. Swimming pool

LEFT: *In the rear, entrance gate to swimming pool area.*
BELOW: *Garden plan.*
RIGHT: *A Japanese maple in raised bed. The entrance to living room is visible beyond.*

Gorman Residence

Leesburg, Virginia

FAR LEFT: *The driveway in autumn.*
ABOVE: *A series of shallow stone steps and landings lead from the driveway to the front door.*

The owners cherished the rural setting of their country home set in the gentle rolling Virginia landscape of undulating grasslands with groves of trees, however the terrain did not respond to all the requirements of an active family with a love of the outdoors. They needed level spaces for ball games, scouting meets and entertaining. While early on the owners stated they were not gardeners and were not interested in creating a garden out of the sixteen acres, they recognized the importance of managing the woodlands to preserve its valuable stands of hardwoods. They sought a plan that would provide for their family's recreational requirements without disturbing the natural beauty of the land.

The approach to the house had to be altered first. The entrance to the driveway from the road was hard to locate and the original driveway led to the back door instead of the front. Rustic stone pillars and low stone walls were added to mark the entrance into the property and now a curving gravel driveway provides a gracious approach to the front entrance before continuing on to a generous parking and service area at the rear of the house.

The house sited at the crest of a treeless rise, with its steep flight of steps leading to the front door, seemed to protrude uncomfortably into the landscape. The house has now been anchored to the ground by installing a series of terraced shallow stone steps and landings interspersed with planting. The Arts and Crafts railings and pillars, designed in tandem with the architect, frame the front entry porch which was widened and paved with diagonally-laid flagstones. Facing west, the porch has become the family's place of choice for relaxing and observing the distant view of rolling hills and stunning sunsets.

The decision of where to locate a field large enough to play ball games was made after reviewing the topography of the property. The only extensive level area was in the middle of the woods. Clearing trees seemed more sensitive to the land and less intrusive than building retaining walls, so a 190-foot-by-90 foot field was carved out of the woods and laid with turf grass. Split log benches, placed around the field's perimeter, define its boundaries and also provide seating for spectators. Large enough to accommodate a variety of games and outdoor activities, this green field has become the focus of many family, community and company gatherings. In the shade of the trees is an open fire pit for cook-outs and is where a rough-hewn Adirondack arbor is located for open air entertaining. From here trails sited through the woods are an invitation for a jog or a quiet stroll.

Finally a planting program was undertaken to supplement the existing stands of maples, oaks, tulip poplars and sweet gum. The addition of Eastern white pines and American hollies provide an evergreen foil to the fiery fall colors of the hardwoods. To add to the joys of spring, flowering trees such as redbuds *(Cercis canadensis)*, Virginia fringe tree *(Chionanthus virginicus)*, and smokebush *(Cotinus coggyria)* were randomly placed throughout, and Yoshino cherries and dogwoods selected to grace the driveway.

The challenges of this project were to provide the amenities that would respond to the family's lifestyle and at the same time enhance the natural charms of the land. The playing field has become the focus of many gatherings. This simple open space surrounded by woods whose colors change from lush green in summer to vivid autumnal tints presents a spectacular scene all year round. The curving driveway adds emphasis to the gentle contours of the land and the approach to the front door with its easy steps and colorful plantings now invites and welcomes the visitor.

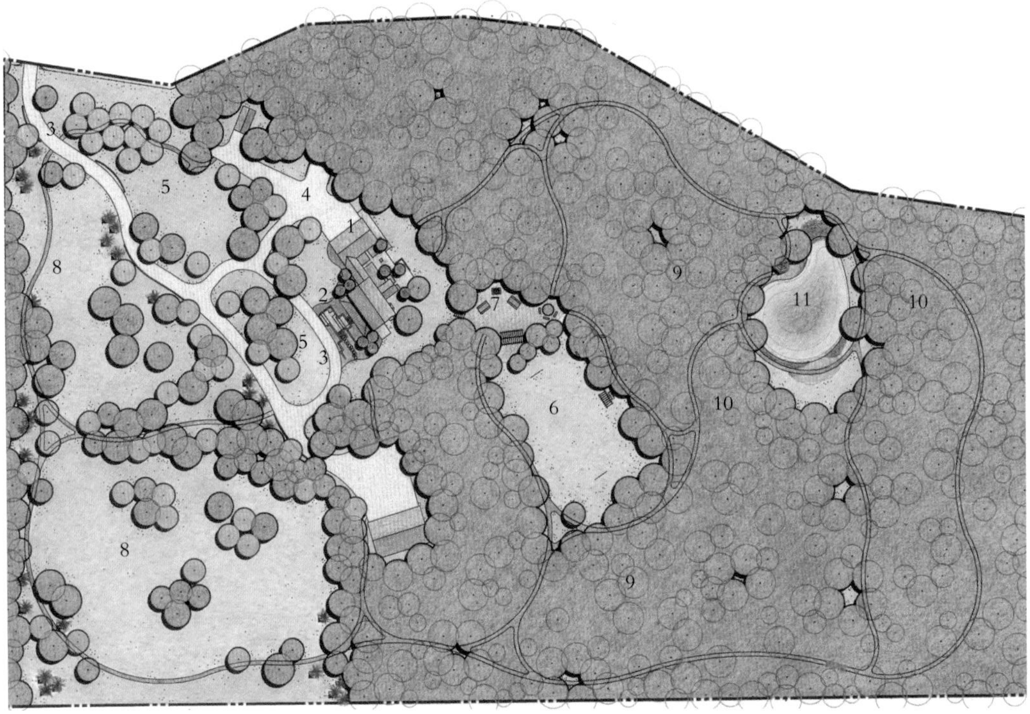

1. House
2. Front entrance steps
3. Driveway
4. Parking and Service area
5. Lawn area
6. Playing field with turf grass
7. Picnic area, arbor and firepit
8. Open grassland
9. Woods
10. Trail
11. Future pond and gazebo

LEFT: *Master plan.*
TOP: *Woodland trail crossing a bridge.*
ABOVE: *Sketch of bridge.*
TOP RIGHT: *Driveway in the summer.*
RIGHT: *Fire pit with split log benches.*

BELOW: *Adirondack arbor with covering of honeysuckle vines (Lonicera sempervirens).*

BELOW: *The playing field in spring.*

ABOVE: *Path mown through a field of long grass.*
RIGHT: *Open grassland.*

McNair Garden

Arlington, Virginia

Design difficulties did not deter these clients from purchasing a charming old house in a leafy neighborhood of Arlington, Virginia, perched atop a steep hill without vehicular access to the street below. The old driveway was lost when the property was subdivided into three lots, leaving the house in the center parcel. An added problem: the city did not allow parking at any time on the street below.

The constraints of the site were formidable. Creative solutions were needed to resolve the complexities of this steep and narrow lot. To bring a driveway straight up from the street with a grade of seventeen percent was unacceptable and impossible to negotiate in icy weather. The solution was to re-grade the slope to accept a serpentine driveway. The result was a graceful driveway that curves around the hill ending in a parking court with seat walls. From this court, which is spacious enough for three or more cars, circular stone steps lead up to the front door. The garage door was relocated to face the new entrance from the street. The concrete surface of the driveway was colored an earth tone to relate to the tan and brown of the stone retaining walls.

The steep slopes between the curves of the driveway, retained by walls of West Virginia stone, are now cloaked in a rich planting of shrubs, such as deutzia 'Nikko', 'Annabelle' hydrangeas, deciduous azaleas, 'Buttercup Winterhazel' (*Corylopsis pauciflora*), anchored by a dwarf Hinoki Cypress (*Chamaecyparis obtusa nana gracilis*). Perennials such as hostas, astilbes, campanulas, chrysanthemums anemones, and annuals such as petunias lend color and interest throughout the year. The density of the planting prevents erosion of the soil on this steep slope. 'Forest Pansy' redbuds line the driveway. It has become a multi-seasonal landscape that commands attention from the street below. A pedestrian path of boulder steps, with its post and rope railing placed amongst the plantings, lead to the entrance court.

The land levels off at the rear of the house making possible the creation of an inviting gar-

LEFT: *Approaching the front door, plantings cascade over the retaining wall.*
ABOVE: *Entering the driveway, the house is glimpsed through the lush plantings.*

den of lawn framed with dogwoods, rhododendrons, hydrangeas and shade-loving perennials such as astilbes, heucheras, ferns and hellebores. Through large French doors the living room flows out onto a flagstone patio with a pergola at one end. Now covered with climbing roses and clematis, it provides effective privacy and screening from the adjacent house.

This project received a Merit Award from the Potomac Chapter of the American Society of Landscape Architects.

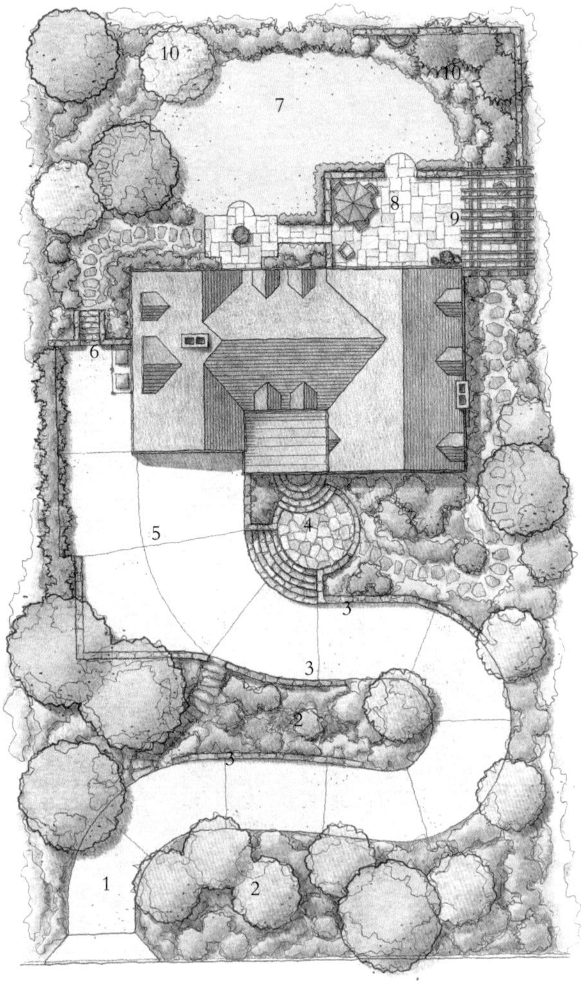

1. Driveway
2. Steep slopes with dense plantings
3. Retaining walls of Western Maryland stone
4. Circular stone entry landing
5. Parking court
6. Steps to rear garden
7. Level lawn surrounded by border of trees shrubs and perennials
8. Terrace
9. Pergola
10. Planted areas

ABOVE LEFT: *Section.*
FAR LEFT: *Garden plan.*
LEFT: *Sketch of the house.*
ABOVE: *At a curve in the driveway, roses and oakleaf hydrangeas in full bloom greet the visitor.*
RIGHT: *The driveway is framed by 'Forest Pansy' redbuds.*

BELOW: *Stone steps ascend to a broad circular landing before continuing to the front door.*

BELOW: *Boulder steps descend through plantings to the entrance.*
FOLLOWING PAGES: *View of the rear garden from beneath the terrace pergola. The seat walls are framed with anemones 'Honorine Jobert'. The bronze foliage of a dogwood highlights the background.*

Bronfman Garden

Washington, DC

The inspiration and focus of this urban condominium garden is a pair of bronze dancing foals poised on a boulder set in a shallow stream. The design was guided by the client's desire to create an appropriate garden setting for her cherished sculpture by the German Expressionist artist, Gerhard Marcks. Designing a garden to feature a work of art is a challenge.

The site was a barren, exposed area with crumbling paving and neglected shrubs; its shape long and rectangular with a depressing flatness. The design addressed this problem by creating a garden on two levels. Low, wide and gentle steps create a comfortable transition between the change in levels. The limestone in the steps matches the capstones of the walls, and the edging of the planting beds serves as a unifying detail throughout the overall design.

A once desolate space has been transformed into a quiet oasis shielded from the street by a high brick wall. Shade trees, an open lawn edged with shrubs and perennials, and a generous terrace now provide a serene setting for enjoying the outdoors and the changing seasons while showcasing this handsome sculpture. From every window there is a garden view. In the shaded areas there are astilbes, helleborus, heuchera, hostas and painted ferns; with peonies, roses, platycodon and iris in the sunny areas. Shrubs against the outside garden wall are underplanted with spring bulbs. The blooms of a Star magnolia dominate the early spring followed by a Meyer's lilac whose fragrance fills the air.

The library leads out to a small circular terrace screened by Japanese maples, a perfect place to read a book in quiet seclusion. The living room opens at the same level on to the main terrace creating a strong connection to the outdoors. Paved with diagonally laid-flagstone, it is shaded by a tall Yellowood tree, which lends a feeling of enclosure and intimacy. Surrounding seat walls retain planting beds where azaleas and espaliered camellias flourish. From the terrace there is an uninterrupted view across the elevated lawn to the rearing foals which appear framed in the arching foliage of the Japanese maples, lush green in the summer and fiery red in fall. A thin sheet

FAR LEFT: *A Japanese maple in fall color creates a canopy over the limestone steps that lead from terrace to garden. Visible to the left is a glimpse of the library terrace with its identifying planters.*

ABOVE: *Sculpture of dancing foals by Gerhard Marcks in place on boulder in the stream bed.*

of water flows over the hooves of the foals, giving the impression they are playing in a mountain stream. This shallow, gently moving stream with its partially exposed river stones has become a favorite destination for birds, much to the client's delight. A tall Sophora tree and surrounding Japanese pines complete the scene.

Light and shade play their parts in this garden design. From the leafy shadows of the terrace, the sunlight of the lawn and garden area appears in brilliant contrast. A barren and neglected urban space has vanished into a tranquil and restful refuge and a natural setting for the prancing colts.

BELOW: *Garden Plan.*
RIGHT: *Library terrace with view through Japanese maple to dining terrace.*

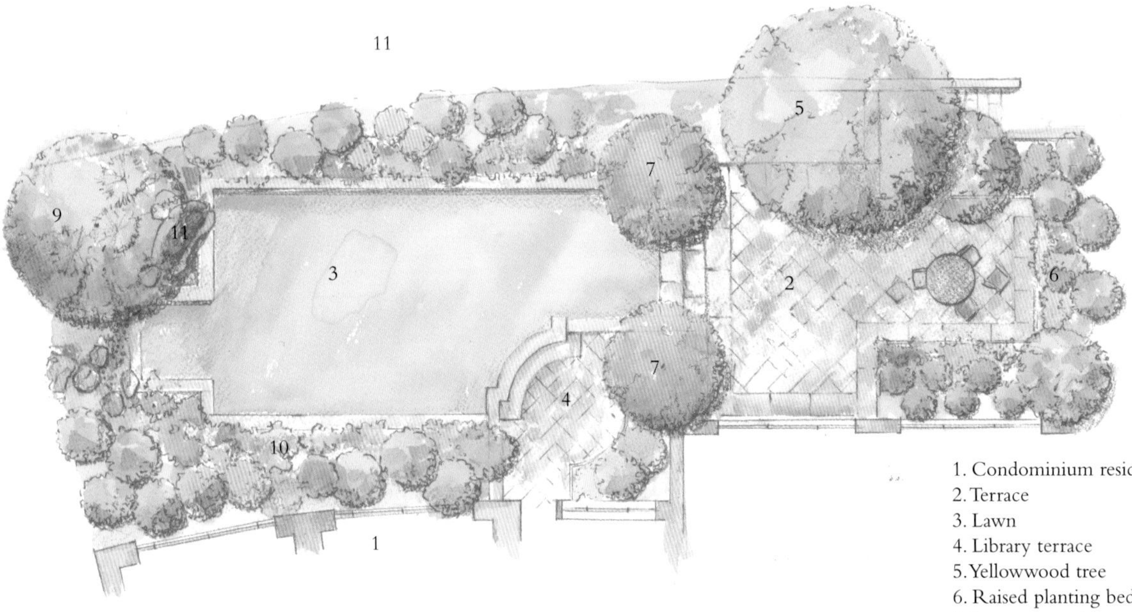

1. Condominium residence
2. Terrace
3. Lawn
4. Library terrace
5. Yellowwood tree
6. Raised planting beds
7. Japanese maple
8. Sculpture
9. Scholar Tree
10. Planting bed
11. Street

BELOW: *Looking back from lawn to terrace framed by Japanese maples in fall color.*

BELOW: *Sculpture as seen across the lawn from the library terrace.*
FOLLOWING PAGES: *The sculpture framed in fall foliage is the focal point viewed from the terrace.*

Mathis Garden

Washington, DC

LEFT: *In the spring, tulips, candytuft and dianthus greet the visitor on arrival at the top of the entrance steps.* ABOVE: *Planting bed outside kitchen door.*

This traditional brick colonial sits on a typical small lot in an inner suburb of Washington, DC. To include all the features the clients desired in this restricted space was a challenge. They wanted the narrow and barren entry court, reached from the street up a flight of steps, to be become a place of welcome, and the unkempt unused rear garden transformed into a livable space with a swimming pool and a terrace for outdoor dining. The design succeeded in addressing both areas of concern with dramatic results.

Now, a new, level entry garden framed by a pair of Service Berry trees, *Amelanchier arborea,* awaits the visitor. It is laid out as a semi-formal parterre with gravel paths and geometric beds on either side of a brick landing that leads to the front door. These small beds with a crisp stone edging, are filled with lavender, germander, grey and green santolina, dwarf Drift roses, candytuft and dianthus. At one end, a small stone bench is backed by Sky Pencil hollies, while a weeping cherry tree provides the other focal point.

Approaching the rear garden at the end of a narrow side path, the gate opens to reveal a vibrant and fully functional family garden quietly tucked behind the house. It is a compact composition that has used every available inch to accommodate a swimming pool, an outdoor shower, a generous terrace, a pool house, a lawn and plantings. The dilapidated garage was transformed, by the architect of the house, into an elegant pool house in the classical style. Once an exposed and unused eyesore to its owners, this rear garden has now become an inviting and livable place with an air of order and repose.

The family room and kitchen open easily through French doors onto the terrace with a pergola at one end and a built-in barbecue at the other. Shallow steps lead up to the swimming pool. Where the ground rises on the north side of the property, low stone retaining walls create planting beds of roses and perennials. Crapemyrtles are espaliered against the white lattice fence, which creates a pleasing foil for their vivid colors. Where the pool deck meets the fence, narrow

planting beds set into the stone paving are planted with peonies and punctuated with narrow upright Graham Blandy boxwoods. When in bloom these beds make a delightful background for the soft grey blue of the pool.

The lawn is a circle of green flush with the pool deck. Between the lawn and the terrace walls are planting beds of bright summer perennials, which soften the stone edges of the terrace walls. At the rear end of the pool, a line of hornbeams provides an aerial privacy screen. The fence was an important design element in establishing the style of the garden. A solid board structure would have created a strong sense of enclosure in this small garden, whereas the open character of lattice lets in light and air, provides sufficient privacy and is an attractive back-drop for the plantings.

This once desolate and rejected area has become the scene of lively social gatherings, family activities, and a continual source of pleasure to its owners.

1. House
2. Steps to Street
3. Terraced planting beds
4. Entry court & parterre garden
5. Side path
6. Terrace
7. Pool
8. Pergola
9. Pool house
10. Lawn
11. Planting bed with crapemyrtles
12. Hornbeam hedge

LEFT: *Garden plan.*
RIGHT: *View of rear garden from above.*

BELOW: *Spring tulips and 'Graham Blandy' boxwoods frame one side of the pool. Fastigiate hornbeams at the rear create an aerial hedge.*

RIGHT: *The BBQ adjacent to the kitchen is tucked in against the stone wall which retains planting beds of perennials and shrubs.*

BELOW: *View from above of the pool and pergola.*

ABOVE: *Echinaceas, coreopsis, 'Moonbeam,' iris cristata, gaura, angelonia and white Wave petunias add summer color. Against the fence, a stone wall retains bed with Crapemyrtles, roses and nepeta.*

RIGHT: *In early fall, sedum 'Autumn Joy,' pennisetum 'Hamlin,' euphorbia 'Diamond Frost,' and angelonia bloom at the path's edge. Shrub with bronze foliage in the rear is Weigela 'Midnight Wine.'*

Hufbauer Revelle Garden

Bethesda, Maryland

This large 1920's house, shaded by old trees, was built on a rise that sloped sharply away from the house. The living room, dining room and kitchen were aligned along the rear axis of the house where the steep topography was a deterrent to stepping into the garden.

To relate the house to the land and to create a seamless transition to the outdoors, a spacious terrace was added that runs the length of the house. The shallow steps at either end lead to the living room and kitchen and provide comfortable circulation throughout. The house and garden is further unified by a stone staircase, centered on the terrace, which descends to a broad sweep of lawn and the deep shade of mature trees.

The terrace has subtle wall lighting, a gentle trickle of water in a niche fountain, seat walls, ample room for outdoor dining and social gatherings, and is lightly shaded by the canopy of an old cherry tree and 'Natchez' crape myrtles. This inviting outdoor living area has added another dimension to the home and become the focus for entertaining and many family activities.

FAR LEFT: *Terrace in spring with canopy of cherry blossoms.*
ABOVE: *View of terrace with* 'Natchez' *Crape Myrtles in bloom.*
BELOW: *A sketch of the niche wall fountain.*

League Roof Garden

Rosslyn, Virginia

LEFT: *View across the Potomac to the Washington Monument. In the foreground a fall mixture of Sedum 'Autumn Joy', Agastache, Gauras and salvia. among grey leaved lavender, santolina and thyme.*
ABOVE: *'Russian Olive' (Eleagnus angustifolia) and 'Inkberry' (Ilex glabra) form a green background for the yellow blooms of daylily 'Happy Returns'. In the corner, a Hollywood Junper gives vertical accent.*

This terrace roof garden in Rosslyn, Virginia is on direct axis with the Washington Monument and commands a stunning and panoramic view of the nation's capital across the Potomac River. When the owner first moved into her new townhouse, she wanted her roof to become a garden at its peak for her annual the 4th of July party—a perfect setting for guests to view the fireworks display.

Because the roof terrace sits atop a wood frame building, weight limits were a major consideration in developing the design. The concept was to create a garden that was a marriage of "green roof" and container planting. Planting beds were laid out using a light weight soil mix that varied in depth from three inches for the shallow rooted plants, to a depth of nine inches sufficient to sustain perennials and shrubs. Beneath these carefully laid out beds the engineering components required for a "green roof" garden were meticulously arranged. The containers with soil deep enough to sustain evergreen shrubs form a backdrop for the beds and provide a sense of enclosure for the garden. Due to restrictions imposed by the homeowners association, it was not possible to have any plantings or structures higher than forty-two inches.

Flagstones set on pedestals allow for drainage and provide a level surface above the uneven floor of the roof deck. A central panel of diagonally-laid pavers anchored by an urn fountain is framed in a band of contrasting granite. A fully-equipped kitchen offers the resources needed for easy entertaining.

Now completely hidden by foliage, the containers hold yews, inkberry and eleagnus forming an evergreen background year round. In spring, dianthus, sedums and creeping phlox burst into vivid color. Throughout the summer and fall, perennials such as lavenders, asgastache, coreopsis, gauras, salvias, daylilies and cone flowers provide a continuum of bloom. Annuals such as "Wave" petunias, zinnias, angelonias add color to the high summer blooms. But it is the shrubs in the planting beds—caryopteris, deutzias, cotoneasters, barberry "Bagatelle" and Hollywood junipers—that give structure throughout the year. A drip irrigation system was needed to insure the success of this hybrid garden.

A spectacular view emerges as dusk falls and the city turns on its lights. At night, fiber optic "fireflies" between the paver joints sparkle in a random pattern mimicking the stars above. What might have been solely a roof terrace with containers has been transformed into a lush and colorful garden, an open-air setting for relaxing and entertaining.

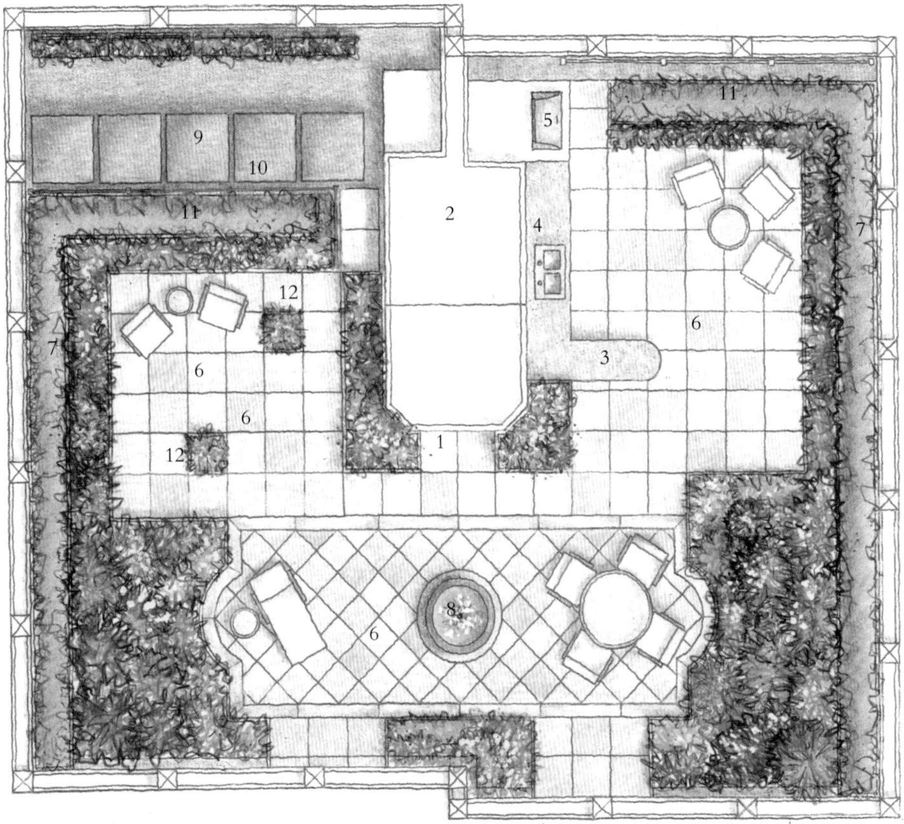

LEFT: *Garden plan.*
ABOVE: *A sketch of the view east to the city from the dining area.*
RIGHT: *Background of Rosslyn high rises with fountain urn in center of terrace. In foreground, planter with summer blooming Mandelvilla vine, juniper and cotoneaster.*

1. Entrance
2. Roof of stairwell
3. Bar
4. Sink
5. BBQ
6. Paving-18 x 18 flagstone on pedestals
7. Yew edge
8. Fountain urn water feature
9. Air conditioners
10. Fence
11. Eleagnus hedge
12. Planting pockets in paving

BELOW: *View across city with spring plantings in bloom among the silver leaved plants.*

BELOW: *Seating area sheltered by yew and eleagnus hedges. In the foreground, dianthus dominates the spring mixture of phlox and salvia among the shrubs.*

McGillivary Garden

Bethesda, Maryland

This comfortable New England style house, set back from the road, is located in an old neighborhood of tall trees and spacious lawns. When the present owners bought the house, the garden had been severely neglected, the plantings overgrown. An addition to the house dramatically changed the relationship of the house to the outdoors and the garden needed significant redesign to accommodate an active young family. They wanted a design that offered space for outdoor living, a swimming pool, a hot tub, a garden with flowers and spaces for children to play.

But before work could begin, a serious drainage problem caused by changes in grade from neighboring construction had to be addressed. A wide and deep swale was made along the edges of the property to divert storm water runoff and carry it out to the main sewer line. At the rear of the house, a sunny, open space was then chosen for the location of a classic rectangular swimming pool and hot tub that were set into a generous flagstone deck. To ensure complete privacy, a row of tall hornbeams creates an aerial hedge behind the pergola that runs the length of the pool. An adjacent pool house, with its gently curved standing-steam copper roof, is fully equipped for entertaining. Access from the house to the pool is easy and fluid. One steps out of the family room to a paved terrace, from which shallow steps at either end lead up to the pool and the hot tub.

From the pool area a stepping stone path placed through beds of roses, dianthus, iris and cranesbill, leads to another small terrace almost hidden away around a corner of the house. The large bay window of the living room overlooks this shaded terrace and across the gently sloping lawn framed by old southern magnolias to the far side of the property. Beneath these trees, shade-loving rhododendrons, hydrangeas, azaleas, hostas, helleborus and ferns flourish. Just a few steps down from the living room, this is a delightfully inviting space for outdoor entertaining.

Beyond this terrace to the side of the house, screened by evergreens, is a small paved basketball court. A handsome wrought iron fence, which separates the court from the front garden, opens out into a densely planted mixed border. Here woody plants such as viburnums, clethras,

FAR LEFT: *October exuberance of Sheffield chrysanthemums offers a spectacular display among perennials and shrubs that frame the path to the front door. In foreground the 'Purple Beauty Bush' , Callicarpa dichotoma, Cranberry cotoneaster , Cotoneaster apiculatus are offset by the autumnal tints of the Oakleaf hydrangea. Hydrangea quercifolia behind.*
ABOVE: *View of house across the lawn.*

deutzias, deciduous azaleas, and winter hazel are interplanted with perennials and annuals such as gauras, anemones, sheffield chrysanthemum, angelonias and scaveolas. This type of planting, which is typical throughout the garden gives, a natural unplanned look and adds colour throughout the season with their sequential blooming.

A stepping stone path leads through this border to a bridge framed by Kousa dogwoods. Crossing the bridge, which straddles the dry streambed of the storm water swale, one arrives at the edge of the large lawn in the foreground of the house. This generous uninterrupted space is ideal for ball games. It is screened by a grand old 'Green Giant' arborvitae hedge which creates not only an effective visual buffer from the road but also provides a dark green background for the brilliant red berries and fall foliage of the 'Winterberry' hollies (*Ilex verticillata*), 'Smoke Bush' (*Cotinus coggygria*), 'Chokeberry' (*Aronia arbutifolia*), viburnums, 'Crimson Pygmy' barberries and sedum 'Autumn Joy.'

The new driveway is of concrete aggregate with a pattern of horizontal bands of flagstone

BELOW: *Garden plan.*
RIGHT: *Bridge spans a dry stream bed.*

1. House
2. Lawn
3. Pool
4. Pergola
5. Pool house
6. Service area
7. Family room terrace
8. Living room terrace
9. Basketball court
10. Fence
11. Bridge
12. Entry terrace
13. Steps
14. Driveway
15. Parking area
16. Planting

and a granite cobblestone edging. In spring, clouds of blossoms from the Yoshino cherries that line the driveway greet the visitor approaching the parking court. From the driveway a flagstone path leads to a spacious entry terrace paved with flagstone in a diagonal pattern and surrounded by seat walls. From this terrace broad curving steps, flanked by a pair of Yellowood trees, flow down to the front lawn. The slopes on either side are densely planted with roses, shrubs and perennials that flower exuberantly from spring through fall.

The redesign brought harmony between the indoor and outdoors, related the new addition to the garden and provided an inviting setting for active family life and entertaining. The garden has responded well to the care of a skilled gardener. It has become a place to wander through and enjoy its vistas, its secluded corners and prolific plantings that provide a variety of changes in foliage and flower throughout the seasons.

BELOW: *Japanese anemones (Honorine Jobert) along the edge of the front lawn with arborvitae hedges behind.*

BELOW: *Deep green of Cryptomerias are a foil for the pure white of 'Annabelle' hydrangeas and the clear yellow of 'Happy Returns' daylilies.*
RIGHT: *Roses, gaura, angelonia, scaveola in summer bloom. As in all beds the planting is a mixture of perennials, shrubs, annuals and bulbs.*

ABOVE: *Entrance path to front door in October.*

RIGHT: *View of swimming pool and hot tub. Planting at edge of pool deck: Boxwood 'Justin Browers,' Juniper procumbens 'Nana,' 'Happy Returns' daylilies and pots of lavender.*

BELOW: *From beneath pergola a view across the lawn of rear garden.*
RIGHT: *Hornbeam trees create a privacy screen. Behind the pergola, shade-loving azaleas, hostas and ferns thrive in beds above low stone retaining walls.*

Taylor Garden

Bethesda, Maryland

FAR LEFT: *Parking bay with gray aggregate paving with bands and edging of Delaware River stone.*
ABOVE: *View of sidewalk garden. A Japanese maple anchors the end of a wide bed planted with shade-loving hydrangeas, azaleas, viburnums, rhododenron, hostas, helleborus and ferns.*

Serenity and an atmosphere of quiet welcome are important when a psychiatrist practices at home. When the owner proposed moving her office to her Bethesda residence, she called on the collaborative efforts of an architect and landscape architect to make the necessary changes to the house and garden. This very small site not only had to accommodate a variety of functions, but also had to maintain a quiet residential character to satisfy the neighbors' objections.

The client, a lover of the outdoors, wanted a private patio where she could sit and quietly read, to be able to view the garden from indoors, and to hear the sound of water splashing outside her office. From a professional standpoint there needed to be a separate entrance for patients, an attractive parking area, and privacy screening from passersby.

The house, a 1940's bungalow, was almost completely hidden behind overgrown shrubbery, the entrance to the front door was through a dilapidated carport, and there was no screening from the street or adjacent houses. The architect's redesign of the house included a large sunny window for the basement-level office. The excavation for its installation created an unsightly hole in the front garden. From challenge to opportunity, this hole was transformed into a shallow pool and waterfall visible from the office. The pool has become a home for a turtle, frogs, and an attraction for visiting birds. The cascading greenery, mossy boulders placed to avert erosion, and the quiet splash of the waterfall provide a peaceful year-round focal point in this small, intimate garden.

The space available for the lower level office entrance on the north side was narrow and limited. For ease of access, the steps were designed with shallow risers and broad landings. Brick planters built on both sides of the steps filled with shade loving plants create a green and inviting approach. A six-foot gray cedar fence, designed to reflect the character of the house, defines the parking area and the new entrance court. It provides privacy for the small patio off the master bedroom and serves as the backdrop for a wide bed of plantings between the residence and the sidewalk. This sidewalk garden offers a seasonal display of color with its profusely planted shrubs and perennials. It has become a focal point of interest on the street and evokes many positive comments.

The home's new main entrance is through a parking court of concrete aggregate edged with Delaware River stone with the same stones curving in bands across it. Together with the extensive new plantings, the fencing screens the cars from all sides.

In the end, the discrete and innovative design matched the client's unique needs and dissipated community concerns.

This project received a Merit Award from the Potomac Chapter of the American Society of Landscape Architects.

BELOW LEFT: *Plan view of the garden.*

BELOW: *Section showing excavation for the office window with small pool and waterfall.*

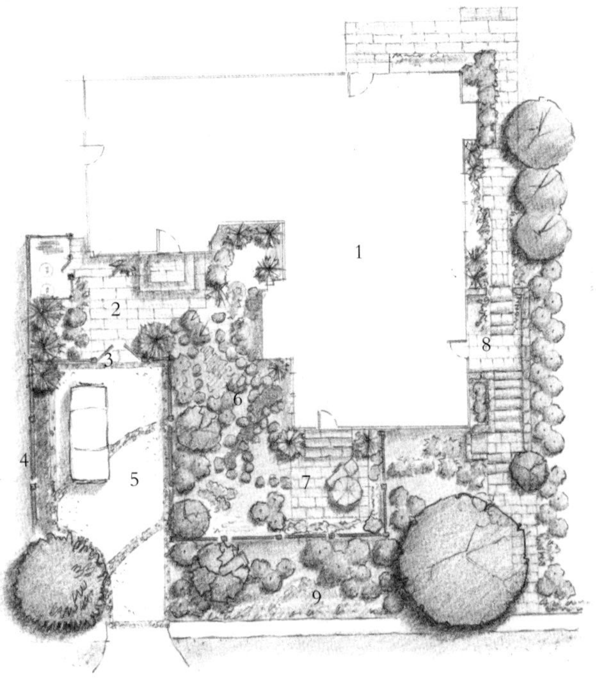

1. Residence
2. Entry court
3. Gate
4. Fence
5. Parking area
6. Garden with pool and waterfall
7. Bedroom patio
8. Office entrance
9. Sidewalk garden

RIGHT: *Entrance gate from parking area.*
BELOW: *Small private patio off master bedroom with a view over the garden.*

ABOVE LEFT: *View of the front entrance to the residence.*

ABOVE: *Hinoki cypress at entrance gate.*

RIGHT: *Waterfall and planting outside office window is designed to remain green throughout the year with plantings of junipers, evergreen ferns, Himalayan box, iris and variegated ivies.*

The American Ambassador's Residence

Islamabad, Pakistan

The Ambassador's residence in Islamabad is situated on a steep hillside commanding a breathtaking view to the foothills of the distant Himalayas. The residence garden, sharing six acres of the thirty-two acre embassy compound, initially consisted of a barren, eroded rocky slope. Surrounded by twelve-foot-high security walls, the site presented extraordinary challenges. Installation of a master plan for the garden was to be phased in several years. The first phase, which began while the residence was still under construction, was the development of the garden.

A spacious lawn for large diplomatic receptions was the most important requirement and an inviting green setting for the house. The design was guided by the need to maximize the dramatic view, screen out the dominating security walls, and establish a sense of privacy and insulation from the busy Chancery nearby.

Previous experience based on years of creating successful gardens in Pakistan, including the garden of the American Consulate in Peshawar, was an important factor in resolving some of the complex challenges that this undertaking presented. First among these was the condition of the site itself, which had been stripped of all vegetation. Erosion had removed all the topsoil and just subsoil remained. The only resource for correcting this was to bring in tons of alluvial soil from the nearby river bed.

Extensive re-grading and terracing of the land was done and a 125-foot-long stone retaining wall constructed to create the large level lawn included in the design. Lacking mechanized equipment, this work was undertaken by laborers helped by young boys who handled the donkeys that valiantly transported the soil, stones and construction materials on and off the site.

The plant selection was determined by the limited supply of viable and acceptable plants available. Existing nursery stock was of poor quality and limited choice. Many of the perennials and all the annuals were propagated by division or from seed. This was done by the gardeners under the

FAR LEFT: *Overview of the garden from the residence.*
ABOVE: *View of the rear terrace with Bauhinia trees.*

supervision of the landscape architect. The extreme summer heat and two months of monsoon rains dictated planting time. Lack of trained labor required constant and intense supervision and, especially important to the client, management of the project budget.

With time, a degraded landscape became a luxuriant green garden with stepped terraces and a large reception lawn. Evergreen hedges of orange trees (*Citrus aurantium*), now screen the ugly security walls and when in bloom, Jacaranda and Bauhinia trees add color and interest to the garden. At the height of summer, the surrounding borders planted with pink and white zinnias, 'Snow in Summer' euphorbia and blue plumbago backed with the hot pink and lilac of the flowering Crepemyrtles, (*Lagerstroemia indica*), make a vivid display against the emerald green of the lawn and are a focal point viewed from the house.

The last phase of the project was the installation of a swimming pool and tennis court which with their noise-generating activities, were located in the farther reaches of the garden. As water was not available in this area, the selection of plants was determined for their drought resistance such as the 'Lemon scented' eucalyptus (*Eucalyptus citriodora*), Indian laburnum (*Cassia fistula*), Bottle Brush shrub (*Callistemon viminalis*), and Australian Silky Oak (*Grevillia robusta*).

Mild winters, hot summers, a regular water supply for the garden and a long growing season make for rapid growth. Without constant vigilance, a garden in this climate soon returns to the wild. Because ambassadors change every two or three years, the fate of the residence garden, given its need for regular maintenance, is ultimately dependent on the interest and funding of its temporary caretakers.

RIGHT: *Grass walk to upper garden terrace.*

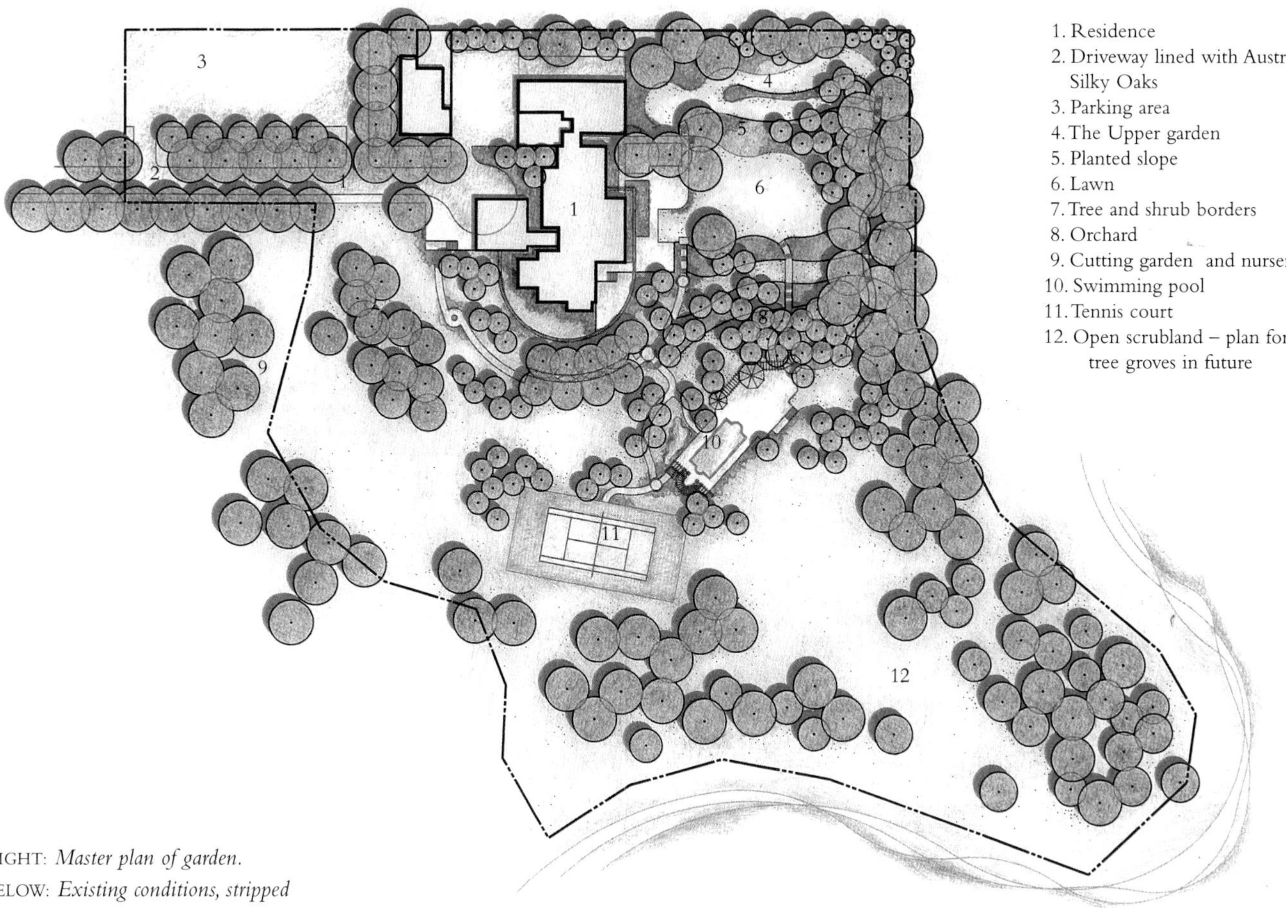

1. Residence
2. Driveway lined with Australian Silky Oaks
3. Parking area
4. The Upper garden
5. Planted slope
6. Lawn
7. Tree and shrub borders
8. Orchard
9. Cutting garden and nursery
10. Swimming pool
11. Tennis court
12. Open scrubland – plan for tree groves in future

RIGHT: *Master plan of garden.*
BELOW: *Existing conditions, stripped of all vegetation and surrounded by a security wall.*

BELOW: *View across rear terrace to the upper garden with Bauhinia trees in bloom in the foreground.*

BELOW: *Steps from rear terrace descend to lawn.*

TOP LEFT: *View across to the hills from the upper garden.*
LEFT: *The upper garden in spring.*

TOP RIGHT: *Flower border in summer..*
LEFT: *Flower border with October asters in bloom.*

RIGHT: *The pool-side pergola as seen from the garden.*
BELOW RIGHT: *Curved steps leading into the swimming pool.*

RIGHT: *Stone steps at the end of the garden flanked by Jacaranda trees connect the upper garden with the lawn below.*
FOLLOWING PAGES: *A Bauhinia tree in bloom at the edge of the terrace; view of the garden from the terrace.*

Firm Profile

Florence Everts Associates is a small, design oriented firm involved in many aspects of landscape architecture in the public and private sectors. Small by intent in order to assure a direct personal and consistent relationship with the client. A responsive working relationship and intense site supervision during installation is we believe, necessary to assure that the final product is an exact reflection of the design concept developed with the client.

As landscape architects we view our role as responsible stewards of the land who are committed to the belief that development of the land must not only serve the needs of the community but also be respectful of its impact on the natural environment.

Florence Everts has received awards from :
Maryland/Potomac Chapter of the American Society of Landscape Architecture for residential work (Florence Everts Associates). As partner in Donnelly, Everts Associates received awards from Prince George's County Real Estate Awards Development Program for Patuxent Place, a mixed use commercial development, Laurel, MD. and American Institute of Architects award for Historic Preservation to Kerns Group architects as landscape architect on team for The Green Door, 16th Street. Washington, DC.

The work of Florence Everts Associates has appeared in *The Washington Post,' Garden Design'* and *'Garden Gate'* magazines; Time Life series *'Gardening in Small Spaces'* & *'Successful Garden Plans"* in *Sunset Northeastern Landscaping Book* ; *'Garden paths: Inspiring Designs and Practical Projects'* and *'Stone in the Garden'* by Gordon Hayward.

Florence Everts Associates

American Embassy Garden of the Ambassador's Residence, Islamabad, Pakistan. Master Plan. Principal designer and construction supervisor of 6-acre garden.

Temple Micah, Cemetery, Washington,DC. Master Plan

Stanford Industrial Park Frederick, MD Fitzgerald Realty Co. Master PlantingPlan

Trinity Episcopal Church , Little Washington, VA. Master Plan.

Tulip Tree Farm, Middleburg, VA. Master Plan for residential area.

The Grass Farm, Markham, VA. Master Plan

Bull Residence, Little Washington ,VA Master Plan

Donnelly, Everts Associates

American Embassy, Islamabad, Pakistan . Master Plan for 32 acre Chancery grounds. Co-author as partner in Donnelly, Everts Associates.

American Embassy, Beijing, China: Site study and Design Recommendations. Co-author as partner in Donnelly, Everts Associates.

National Cathedral School for Girls, Washington,DC.Historic Renovation Hearst Hall. Master Plan . Co-author in Donnelly, Everts Associates. Architect: Notter, Finegold & Alexander.

The Green Door. Renovation of historic Werlich mansion Washington, DC. Landscape architect on Kerns Group Architects team

Professional activities: Instructor Landscape Design Program at George Washington University. Workshops for staff at MNCPPC Brookside Gardens, Md. Juror for Georgetown Garden Days Awards.

Project Credits

Bronfman Residence
Project manager: Florence Everts
Masonry contractor: Jopal Construction
Landscape company: Chapel Valley
Water feature: Washington Water Gardens
Gardener: Peter Schenk

League Roof Garden
Project manager: Florence Everts
Consultants: Seal Engineering: Waterproofing
Structural engineer: James Konnick
General contractor: James Walls and Company
Landscape contractor: Evergro Landscaping, Inc.
Lighting, including fibre optics: C.R.B Electric
Kitchen equipment: Vermont Islands
Gardener: Michael Anderson

McNair Residence
Project Manger: Florence Everts
Architect: Harlan Hadley
Masonry contractor: Jopal Construction
Driveway contractor: Virginia Concrete
Landscaping contractor: Evergro Landscaping, Inc.
Carpentry: Grant Faller
Gardener: Andy Lillycrop

Mathis Residence
Project manager: Florence Everts
Architect: Frederick Tyler
Masonry: Neto Construction
Swimming Pool: Town & Country Pools
Fencing : Brattleworks Inc.
Landscape contractor: Evergro Landscaping, Inc.
Carpentry: Karl Vogelmayer & Co.
Gardener: Lisa Mills

McGillivary Residence
Project manager: Florence Everts
Masonry: Jopal Construction
Swimming Pool: Alpine Pools
Carpentry: Grant Faller
Ironwork: Northeast Iron
Landscape contractor: Evergro landscaping, Inc.
Arborist: Bartlett Tree Co.
Gardener: Lisa Mills

Taylor Residence
Project manager: Florence Everts
Architect: Harlan Hadley
General contractor: Monte Notten Inc.
Landscape contractor: Evergro Landscaping Inc.

Gorman Residence
Project manager: Florence Everts
General Contractor: Oakridge Builders
Masonry: Hurddle Stone Works, Inc.
Landscape contractor: Evergro landscaping Inc.

Residence of the American Ambassador, Islamabad Pakistan
Project manager: Florence Everts
Site work: grading and construction (contractual labor hired by Embassy)
Landscape work: Embassy grounds staff and locally recruited village labor

Hufbauer/Revelle Residence
Project Manager: Florence Everts
Masonry: Jopal Construction
Ironwork: Northeast Iron Works
Landscape contractor: Evergro Landscaping, Inc.

Everts Residence
Stonework: Dan Waters
Carpentry for Tea house: Peter Wechsler, Daiku Woodworking
Stair railing: Ron Paci
Gardener: Michael Anderson

Spencer Residence
Project manager: Florence Everts
Masonry contractor: Serra Stone
Landscape contractor: Evergro Landscaping, Inc.
Carpentry: Barry Potter
Water Feature: Bjoern Neumann
Lighting: C.R.B. Electric

Photo Credits

Roger Foley
Michael Selig
Florence Everts
Don Partlan
Renato Salazar
James Quoyle

Drawing Credits

Dennis Dixon
Susanne Fyffe
Karen Kumm
Wynn Withans
Sharon Bradley Papp